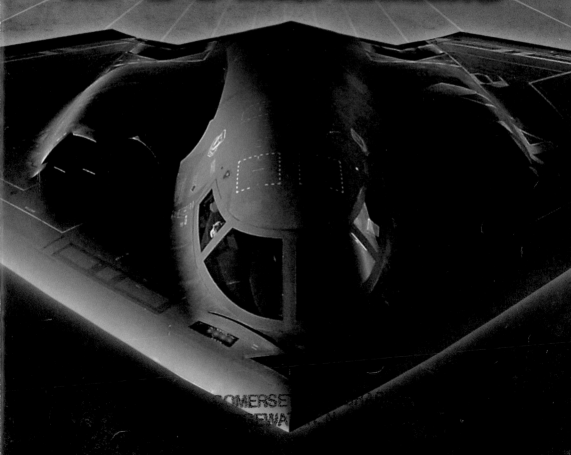

B-2 STEALTH BOMBERS

BY JACK DAVID

BELLWETHER MEDIA · MINNEAPOLIS, MN

Are you ready to take it to the extreme?
Torque books thrust you into the action-packed
world of sports, vehicles, and adventure. These books
may include dirt, smoke, fire, and dangerous stunts.
WARNING: read at your own risk.

Library of Congress Cataloging-in-Publication Data

David, Jack, 1968-
  B-2 stealth bombers / by Jack David.
      p. cm. -- (Torque, military machines)
  Summary: "Explains the technologies and capabilities of the latest generation of military B-2
planes. Intended for grades 3 through 7 "--Provided by publisher.
  Includes bibliographical references and index.
  ISBN-13: 978-1-60014-103-4 (hbk : alk. paper)
  ISBN-10: 1-60014-103-X (hbk : alk. paper)
1. B-2 bomber--Juvenile literature. 2. Stealth aircraft--Juvenile literature. I. Title. II. Series.

  UG1242.B6D376 2008
  623.74'63--dc22

                                                                                          2007012159

This edition first published in 2008 by Bellwether Media.

The photographs in this book are reproduced through the courtesy of: the United States Department of
Defense, front cover, pp. 8-9, 10-11, 12-13, 14-15, 16-17, 18-19, 20-21; Ted Carlson/fotodynamics, pp. 4-5, 6.

CONTENTS

THE B-2 IN ACTION

A strange-looking plane called a B-2 Spirit begins its wartime **mission**. It takes off from Whitman Air Force Base in Missouri. Two pilots fly the plane. The mission will take them halfway around the earth.

The B-2 is a valuable tool. It is built to be almost totally "invisible" to its enemies. This is why it is called a **stealth** bomber. The B-2 flies at top speeds. It can reach its target in just a few hours.

★ FAST FACT ★

The B-2 can fly over 6,000 miles (9,656 kilometers) without refueling.

It's time for the B-2 to complete its mission. The pilots launch two bombs. The bombs cruise down to their targets and explode. The pilots turn the plane around and fly safely back to their base.

STEALTH BOMBER

Bombers in the U.S. military have always done dangerous work. The military uses them to destroy targets such as enemy bases. Enemies have always worked hard to shoot them down. They target bombers from the ground or from other planes.

A new technology changed that. The B-2 is built to be invisible to **radar**. It has no sharp edges or flat surfaces. This shape lets it fly past most radar detectors.

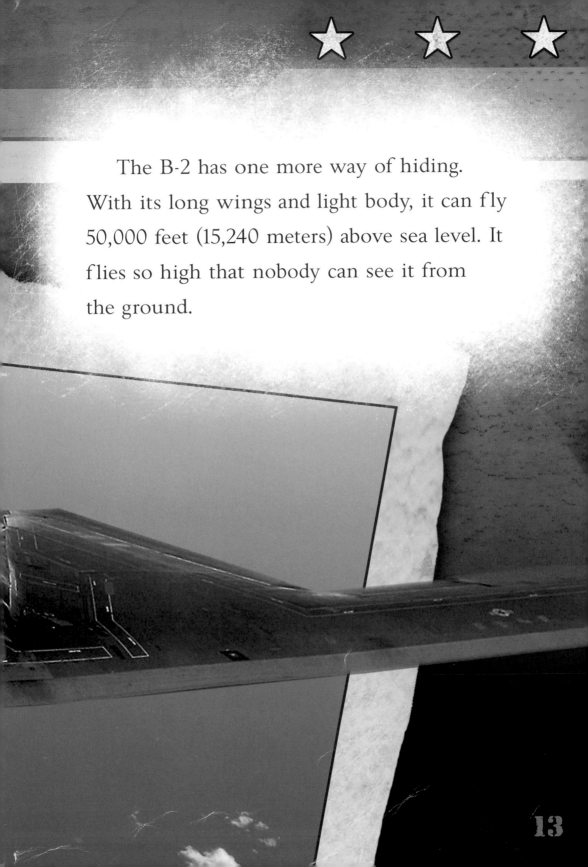

The B-2 has one more way of hiding. With its long wings and light body, it can fly 50,000 feet (15,240 meters) above sea level. It flies so high that nobody can see it from the ground.

WEAPONS

The B-2 can carry a variety of weapons. Its main weapon is the JDAM. This bomb has a guidance system that helps it hit its target. This is why it is called a **"smart bomb."**

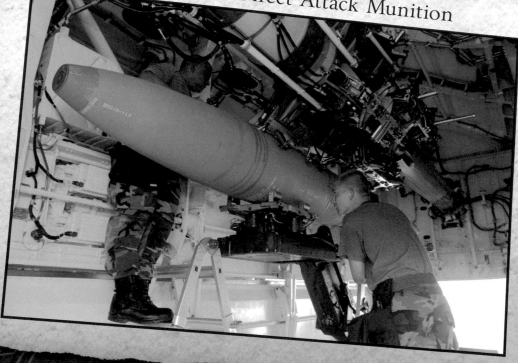

JDAM - Joint Direct Attack Munition

B-2 SPIRIT SPECIFICATIONS:

Primary Function: Multi-role heavy bomber

Length: 69 feet (21 meters)

Height: 17 feet (5 meters)

Wingspan: 172 feet (52 meters)

Speed: Classified

Range: 6,000 miles (9,656 kilometers)

Ceiling: 50,000 feet (15,240 meters)

Weight: 336,500 pounds (152,634 kilograms)

JASSMs - Joint Air-to-Surface Standoff Missiles

B-2s also have JASSMs. The JASSM is a cruise **missile**. It can change direction in flight to follow a moving target.

The B-2 also carries free-fall bombs that have no guidance systems. They cannot change direction once they are launched.

B-2 MISSIONS

Safety is always a concern for the Air Force. B-2 pilots are not in radio contact with anyone. Enemies could detect the radio signals. They could use the signals to find the planes.

★ FAST FACT ★

The B-2 has an average cost of $2.2 billion.

Two pilots prepare for a B-2 mission.

Bombing missions always happen at night. Darkness adds even more protection for the B-2. The pilots can launch their weapons without ever being detected. They are already headed home by the time the weapons hit their target.

GLOSSARY

missile—an explosive launched at targets on the ground or in the air

mission—a military task

radar—a sensor system that uses radio waves to locate objects in the air

smart bomb—a bomb that includes a system that guides it to its target

stealth—hidden

TO LEARN MORE

AT THE LIBRARY

Braulick, Carrie A. *U.S. Air Force Bombers.* Mankato, Minn.: Capstone Press, 2007.

Cooper, Jason. *U.S. Air Force.* Vero Beach, Fla.: Rourke, 2004.

Doeden, Matt. *The U.S. Air Force.* Mankato, Minn.: Capstone Press, 2005.

ON THE WEB

Learning more about military machines is as easy as 1, 2, 3.

1. Go to www.factsurfer.com

2. Enter "military machines" into search box.

3. Click the "Surf" button and you will see a list of related web sites.

With factsurfer.com, finding more information is just a click away.

INDEX